MEET THE WILD THINGS

Hello, I'm a
SLOTH

by Hayley & John Rocco

putnam

G. P. PUTNAM'S SONS

Oh, hiiiiiiiii!

You caught me in the middle of a nap.
But that's okay. It's not hard to do
when I sleep most of the day.

I was actually just thinking about how much
I love trees. In fact, I spend most of my time
in them. I sleep, I eat, I sleep, and I climb.

Don't you just love climbing trees?

My claws act as hooks, which makes it super easy to hang from branches.

Actually, the only time I climb down
to the ground is once a week to poop.

How often do you poop?

I don't stay down for very long because there are animals on the ground that would love to have me for dinner.

Sometimes I fall. Oops!
But don't worry. I can fall up
to 100 feet without getting hurt!

Does it hurt when you fall?

Hmmm. Now I just have to find a good tree
to climb. It can take me a while because
I'm not built for walking on the ground.

But I swim really well. Because of the food
I eat, my stomach fills with gas like a balloon,
helping me to float easily. I use my arms and
legs as oars to propel me through the water.

Can you swim?

When I am high up in the trees, I worry about harpy eagles. They want to eat me, too! Luckily, I grow lots of green algae on my fur, which can make me hard to find—especially when I'm moving so slow.

Scientists have discovered
that the algae and fungi
in my fur can fight certain
human diseases, like cancer.

You're welcome.

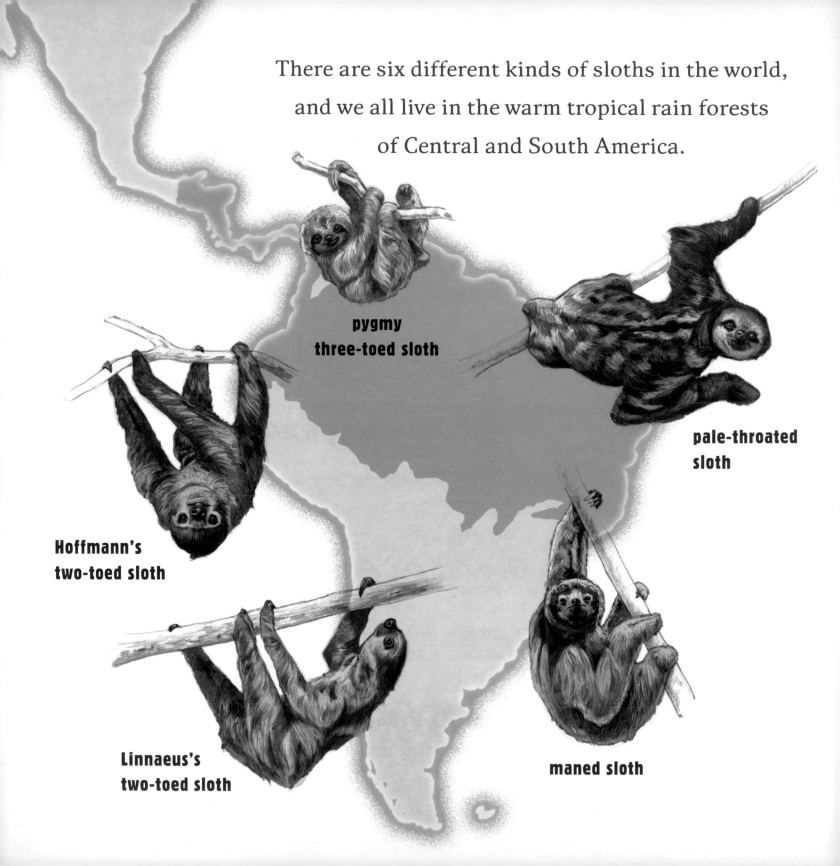

There are six different kinds of sloths in the world,
and we all live in the warm tropical rain forests
of Central and South America.

pygmy
three-toed sloth

pale-throated
sloth

Hoffmann's
two-toed sloth

Linnaeus's
two-toed sloth

maned sloth

I am called a brown-throated three-toed sloth.

Can you guess why?

Most people think I like to keep to myself. But I've got hundreds of friends with me wherever I go.

Many of them are moths and beetles that live in my fur! My favorite are these little guys, called cryptoses moths. They only live on sloths.

Do you have any bugs living on you?

Leaves are pretty much the only thing I eat.
They take a while to digest, and they
don't give me much energy. That's one
of the reasons I move so slow.

What's your favorite food?

I can't see very well, so I move carefully, feeling my way from branch to branch.

But when trees are cut down,
I lose my pathway to other
trees I need for food.

I'm sure you've heard that a lot
of trees have been cut down lately.
And that's made it harder and harder
for us sloths to survive.

Fortunately, there are lots of people who are helping by planting trees and working to protect forests.

In the meantime, they're building rope bridges to help us get to where we need to go.

Will you help, too?

Well, that was a lot of talking,
and I'm pretty tired.
Let's hang out again soon.
Until then, YAWN . . .

Good niiiiiiiight.

A little more about sloths:

- Sloths take a long time to turn their leaf-based diet into energy. It can take them an entire month to digest a single leaf!

- Sloths are masters of disguise. The algae that covers their fur gives them a mossy green color, perfect for hiding in the forest canopy. Predators that use their sense of sight to locate prey, like harpy eagles, often fly right over sloths hanging in plain sight.

- Sloths also have another trick up their sleeves. They don't produce any body odor at all, and because they're covered in algae, they smell just like the jungle. This makes it nearly impossible for predators that use their sense of smell to hunt, like jaguars, to detect them.

- Sloths have special tendons in their hands and feet that can lock into place, allowing them to hang upside down for long periods of time, even while sleeping. Amazingly, sloths spend about 90 percent of their lives hanging upside down. That's a lot of hanging around!

- Prehistoric ground sloths walked on two legs, and the largest, the Megatherium, has been recorded at heights of almost twenty feet. Unfortunately, humans hunted the ground sloths into extinction nearly 11,000 years ago.

- Because there has been little research done, the natural life span of sloths in the wild is currently unknown. They have been known to live a long time in captivity (50+ years), but scientists believe they actually live longer in the wild.

- Sloths have been misunderstood as lazy creatures simply because they move slowly. In fact, in most languages, their name means "lazy." But actually, moving slowly helps sloths go undetected by predators who may be nearby. This technique has worked so well, it's helped sloths survive for nearly 64 million years.

- Sloth claws look like long nails, but they are in fact curved finger bones covered with a sheath of keratin—the same material that makes up human fingernails.

- Sloths cannot regulate their own body heat, so they constantly move in and out of the sun to make sure they are at just the right temperature.

- Sloths contain entire ecosystems of insects, fungi, and algae in their fur. Up to 950 beetles, moths, cockroaches, and even worms can be found on one individual sloth.

Why are sloths endangered?

In Costa Rica alone, wildlife rescue centers receive two or three sloths a day, representing almost half of all mammals admitted across the country.

Habitat loss due to human development impacts the sloths' corridors, or pathways through the trees. This forces sloths to climb down to the ground, where they are most vulnerable to being hit by vehicles or targeted by predators or poachers. A poacher is a person who hunts or captures animals illegally to make money.

Sloths are also constantly at risk of electrocution as they attempt to use power lines to go from one location to another.

One of the greatest threats to sloths is exploitation for selfies—sloth babies are stolen from their mothers by poachers because tourists will pay for the opportunity to take photos with them. Unfortunately, these sloths are not cared for properly and cannot survive without their mothers.

Organizations working to help sloths:

The Sloth Conservation Foundation: SlothConservation.org
The Sloth Institute: TheSlothInstitute.org
World Wildlife Fund: WorldWildlife.org/species/sloth

brown-throated three-toed sloth

©Hayley Rocco

 For more information about sloths and how you can help them, visit
MeetTheWildThings.com

For my friend, Sarah Jane. —H.R.

For Cecilia Yung. —J.R.

HAYLEY AND JOHN ROCCO are both ambassadors for Wild Tomorrow, a nonprofit focused on conservation and rewilding South Africa. They are the author and illustrator team behind the picture book *Wild Places: The Life of Naturalist David Attenborough*. John is also the #1 *New York Times* bestselling illustrator of many acclaimed books for children, some of which he also wrote, including *Blackout*, the recipient of a Caldecott Honor, and *How We Got to the Moon*, which received a Sibert Honor and was longlisted for the National Book Award. Learn more at MeetTheWildThings.com.

ACKNOWLEDGMENTS We would like to thank Dr. Rebecca Cliffe of the Sloth Conservation Foundation in Costa Rica for sharing her expertise and guidance during the creation of this book. We would also like to thank the inspiring people of Costa Rica who passionately shared their knowledge with us as we searched for and studied sloths in the wild.

G. P. PUTNAM'S SONS | An imprint of Penguin Random House LLC, New York
First published in the United States of America by G. P. Putnam's Sons, an imprint of Penguin Random House LLC, 2024

Text copyright © 2024 by Hayley Rocco | Illustrations copyright © 2024 by John Rocco

Penguin supports copyright. Copyright fuels creativity, encourages diverse voices, promotes free speech, and creates a vibrant culture. Thank you for buying an authorized edition of this book and for complying with copyright laws by not reproducing, scanning, or distributing any part of it in any form without permission. You are supporting writers and allowing Penguin to continue to publish books for every reader. | G. P. Putnam's Sons is a registered trademark of Penguin Random House LLC. | The Penguin colophon is a registered trademark of Penguin Books Limited. | Visit us online at PenguinRandomHouse.com.

Library of Congress Cataloging-in-Publication Data | Names: Rocco, Hayley, author. | Rocco, John, illustrator. | Title: Hello, I'm a sloth / written by Hayley Rocco; illustrated by John Rocco. | Other titles: Hello, I am a sloth | Description: New York: G. P. Putnam's Sons, 2024. | Series: Meet the wild things; 1
Summary: "An introduction to the unique characteristics of the sloth"—Provided by publisher. | Identifiers: LCCN 2023009818 (print)
LCCN 2023009819 (ebook) | ISBN 9780593618127 (hardcover) | ISBN 9780593618141 (kindle edition) | ISBN 9780593618134
Subjects: LCSH: Sloths—Juvenile literature. | Classification: LCC QL737.E2 R63 2024 (print) | LCC QL737.E2 (ebook) | DDC 599.3/13—dc23/eng/20230308
LC record available at https://lccn.loc.gov/2023009818 | LC ebook record available at https://lccn.loc.gov/2023009819

ISBN 9780593618127 | 10 9 8 7 6 5 4 3 2 1
Manufactured in China | TOPL

Design by Nicole Rheingans | Text set in Narevik | The art was created with pencil, watercolor, and digital color.
The publisher does not have any control over and does not assume any responsibility for author or third-party websites or their content.